Metallic GLAM Nail Studio

BY THE
EDITORS
OF KLUTZ

KLUTZ®

CONTENTS

Gum
Balls
9

Gold
Coin
9

Star
Light
10

Zodiac
Sign
11

Secret
Agent
12

Mer-mazing Scales
15

Confetti Sprinkles
16

Rainbow Connection
18

Paint Brush
20

Tropical Leaves
22

Dream Garden
24

Paw Prints
27

Cute Pup
27

Wagging Tail
27

Ice Pop
28

Beachy Waves
29

Sparkly Starfish
29

Dazzling Desert
30

Tiny Heart
32

Boho Arrows
33

Fancy Feather
33

Gorgeous Galaxy
34

Slime Time
37

Mysterious Moon
38

New Moon
39

Ombré Shimmer
40

Fresh Fruit
42

Watermelon Rind
43

Stunning Sunset
45

Unicorn Magic
46

WHAT YOU GET

AVOIDING SPILLS
Nail polish is difficult to remove, so avoid spilling it at all costs! Cover your work surface with a protective layer, like a plastic tablecloth. Make sure that your polish bottles won't get knocked over while you're painting.

Nail polish in 6 colors

DISCO FLAMINGO · Nail Polish · Net Wt. 0.17 oz (5 mL)

CITRUS SUPREME · Nail Polish · Net Wt. 0.17 oz (5 mL)

FAB FUCHSIA · Nail Polish · Net Wt. 0.17 oz (5 mL)

COSMIC CRUSH · Nail Polish · Net Wt. 0.17 oz (5 mL)

SNOW BUNNY · Nail Polish · Net Wt. 0.17 oz (5 mL)

PIXIE DUST · Nail Polish · Net Wt. 0.17 oz (5 mL)

Polish blender

2-in-1 detail brush tool

IT'S A GOOD IDEA TO HAVE THESE SUPPLIES ON HAND, TOO:

NAIL POLISH REMOVER

COTTON BALLS

PETROLEUM JELLY

COTTON SWABS

PAPER TOWELS

Foil nail stickers

REMOVING POLISH
When you've had enough of your nail art, use nail polish remover to wipe it away. You can find nail polish remover at your local drugstore.

PREP YOUR NAILS

Nails are the perfect blank canvas to create tiny works of art. For the best results, start your manicure by cleaning and smoothing your nails just a bit.

❶ CLEAN

Remove any old polish with a cotton ball dipped in nail polish remover. Wash your hands with warm, soapy water, making sure to get any dirt lurking under your nails.

❷ TRIM

With the nail clippers, trim your nails to the same length. Try to create a nice, rounded shape.

❸ FILE

Rub a nail file lightly under each nail at an angle. Gently file in long strokes in one direction. Do not file back and forth (that will damage your nails).

❹ MOISTURIZE

Work a bit of lotion into your hands. Let it dry before painting your nails.

YOU WILL NEED

Nail polish remover + cotton balls (optional)

Nail brush

Nail clippers

Nail file

Lotion

PAINT A BASE COAT

Lay down a basic layer to make your designs pop!

1 Unscrew the cap and carefully lift the polish brush. At the same time, wipe the side of the brush against the inside of the bottle lip. You don't want too much polish on your brush—just a thin coat.

2 Place your finger flat on the table. Starting at the base of your nail, paint a stripe up the middle.

3 Paint another stripe on the left side of your nail. . .

. . . and a stripe on the right side.

4 Repeat Steps 1–3 if the base coat is looking thin. Then let it dry completely (about 10–15 minutes).

> **··· PRO TIP ···**
> When your polish starts to look chipped, remove it with nail polish remover.

USING YOUR TOOL

When you need to paint details, this is your go-to helper!

The tool has two ends:

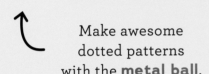

Make awesome
dotted patterns
with the **metal ball**.

Use the **small brush** to
paint thin details like
flower stems.

USING THE NAIL STICKERS

Peel and stick a nail sticker to a
(dry) colored nail. It adds flair
without a lot of work!

MAKING A PALETTE

1 Fold a piece of paper
in half, and blob
a little bit of nail
polish on the paper.

2 Dip one end of your tool
into the polish. When
the polish starts to dry
on the palette, add a
fresh drop.

··· PRO TIP ···
Wipe polish from the tool using nail polish
remover before you switch colors.

GLITZY GUM BALLS

Bring on the bling!

SUGGESTED COLORS

1 Paint a white base coat (page 6) on your nails.

2 GUM BALLS
Using the dotting tool, paint pink dots on some of your nails.

3 Let the polish dry a bit before you switch colors. Then, dab some green on dots your nail.

4 Repeat Step 3 with blue, then purple polish. Lookin' sweet!

5 GOLD COIN
Paint a gold circle in the center of your nail. Use the detail brush, and work slowly to get a perfect circle.

6 Once the gold is dry, use the detail brush and blue polish to paint a cent sign. Draw a C first, then a straight line.

MANI STYLE BOX

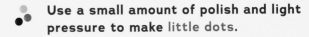

ACCENT NAIL
Leave one nail plain white, so you can add the gumball machine sticker.

DOTS, DOTS, DOTS!

You can make dots of different sizes using the same tool!

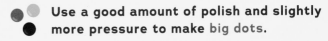

Use a small amount of polish and light pressure to make little dots.

Use a good amount of polish and slightly more pressure to make big dots.

Make a dot, then pull one edge out with the brush to make a teardrop.

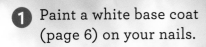

STAR LIGHT

Keep it simple with easy-breezy decals.

SUGGESTED COLOR

You will also need the sticker sheet.

WHAT'S YOUR SIGN?

1 STARS
Paint a pink base coat (page 6) on your nails.

2 Let the paint dry completely. Then place one or two star stickers on each nail.

3 ZODIAC SIGN
Practice painting your symbol on a piece of scrap paper.

4 Use gold polish to paint your symbol on your nail.

5 To help your stickers stay on longer, you can paint clear nail polish over the design.

··· PRO TIP ···
Clear nail polish is the secret to long-lasting nail art. You can find it at any local drugstore. Paint clear polish over your finished (dry) design to seal it.

ARIES
March 21 –
April 19

TAURUS
April 20 –
May 20

GEMINI
May 21 –
June 21

CANCER
June 22 –
July 22

LEO
July 23 –
August 22

VIRGO
August 23 –
September 22

LIBRA
September 23 –
October 23

SCORPIO
October 24 –
November 21

SAGITTARIUS
November 22 –
December 21

CAPRICORN
December 22 –
January 19

AQUARIUS
January 20 –
February 18

PISCES
February 19 –
March 20

SECRET AGENT

Hide a top secret message in plain sight.

1. Paint a blue base coat (page 6) on your nails.

2. While you're waiting for the base coat to dry, decide what you want to spell out in code.

3. With a contrasting color, paint dots and dashes. You can switch colors between nails, if you'd like.

SUGGESTED COLORS

Use the ball end of your tool to make dots.

With the brush end of your tool, draw dashes.

INTERNATIONAL MORSE CODE

The combo of dots and dashes is a way of spelling out messages. Before telephones were invented, people would send messages using a special machine that could tap out letters using this code.

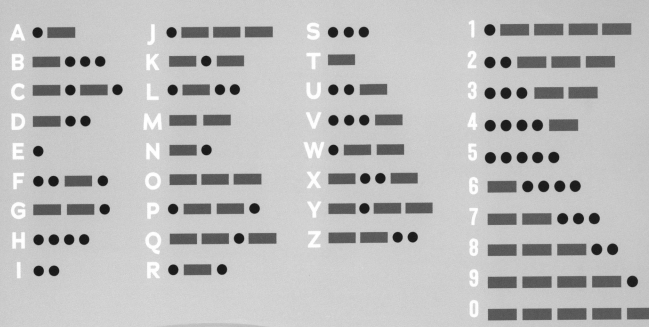

MER-MAZING SCALES

Make a splash with metallics!

SUGGESTED COLORS

1 Paint a purple base coat (page 6) on your nails.

2 Paint two or three blue dots toward the tip of your nail.

3 Add a few dots in gold and purple next to the blue dots to make a row across the nail.

4 Repeat Steps 2–3 to make a row of dots slightly below the first. Overlapping the dots will make them look like scales.

5 Continue making rows of dots in blue, gold, and purple until you run out of room on your nail.

··· **PRO TIP** ···
Mermaid makeovers aren't instant, so take your time with this design.

ACCENT NAIL

Decorate solid-colored nails with a shell, nautilus, or whale tail.

CONFETTI SPRINKLES

Treat yourself to a sugar rush.

SUGGESTED COLORS

1 Paint a pink base coat (page 6) on your nails.

2 With the detail brush, draw a few short blue lines.

ACCENT NAIL

Place a sticker on a plain nail if you *donut* want all sprinkles.

3 Add a few green lines.

4 Finish with some white sprinkles.

COLOR SWITCH
Paint the base coat in any "frosting" color that you'd like. "Vanilla" looks lovely!

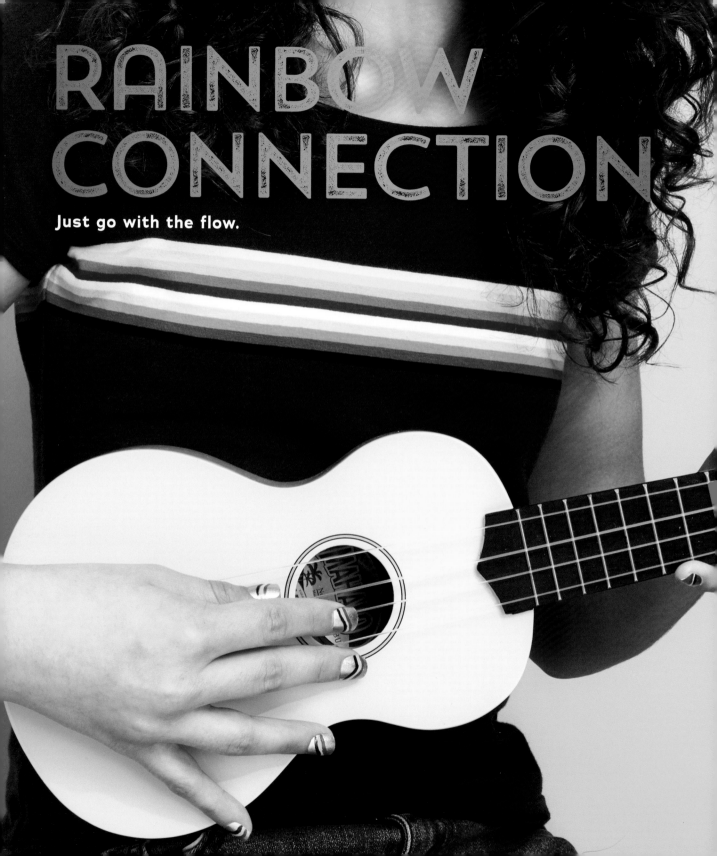

RAINBOW CONNECTION

Just go with the flow.

SUGGESTED COLORS

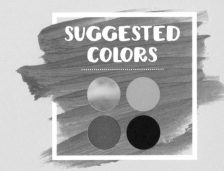

1 Paint a gold base coat (page 6) on your nails.

2 With the detail brush, paint a green wavy line across your nail.

··· PRO TIP ···
Try to paint the line so it looks like it connects across your nails.

3 Add a pink line just above the green line.

··· PRO TIP ···
It's way easier to paint with the hand you write with. Get help from a friend and offer to do their nails, too!

4 Finish by painting a blue line below the green line.

PAINT BRUSH

Express your artistic spirit.

1. Paint a white base coat (page 6) on your nails.

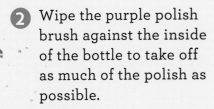

2. Wipe the purple polish brush against the inside of the bottle to take off as much of the polish as possible.

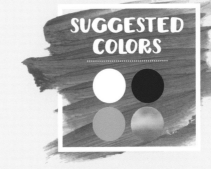

SUGGESTED COLORS

3. Lightly brush random streaks on your nail. Paint some side-to-side, and others up-and-down. You should still be able to see a lot of the white base coat.

4. Repeat Steps 2–3 using green polish.

5. To finish your masterpiece, repeat Steps 2–3 with gold polish.

ACCENT NAIL

Leave one nail blank for the artist brush sticker.

TROPICAL LEAVES

It's a jungle out there.

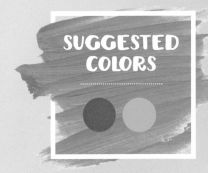
COLOR SWITCH
Feel free to use a purple base coat instead of pink—or mix and match!

1. Paint a pink base coat (page 6) on your nails.

2. Using the detail brush, paint a diagonal green curve across your nail.

3. Add short green lines connecting to the stem.

ACCENT NAIL

Stickers are perfect for leaf-less nails. Try a chic gold triangle, tropical flower, or toucan!

MANI STYLE BOX

DREAM GARDEN

Dark and dramatic florals for your fingertips.

1. Paint a blue base coat (page 6) on your nails.

2. Use the detail brush to paint green leaves.

3 With the dotting tool, add clusters of purple and gold dots to make flowers.

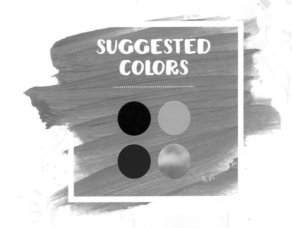

4 Add a gold dot to the center of each purple flower, and a purple dot to each gold flower.

Change the direction of the leaves and flowers as you go, to create interest.

5 Add a few lines and dots in gold or purple to fill in empty spaces.

COLOR SWITCH
Is spring in the air? Swap the blue base coat with white, and paint pink flowers instead of purple.

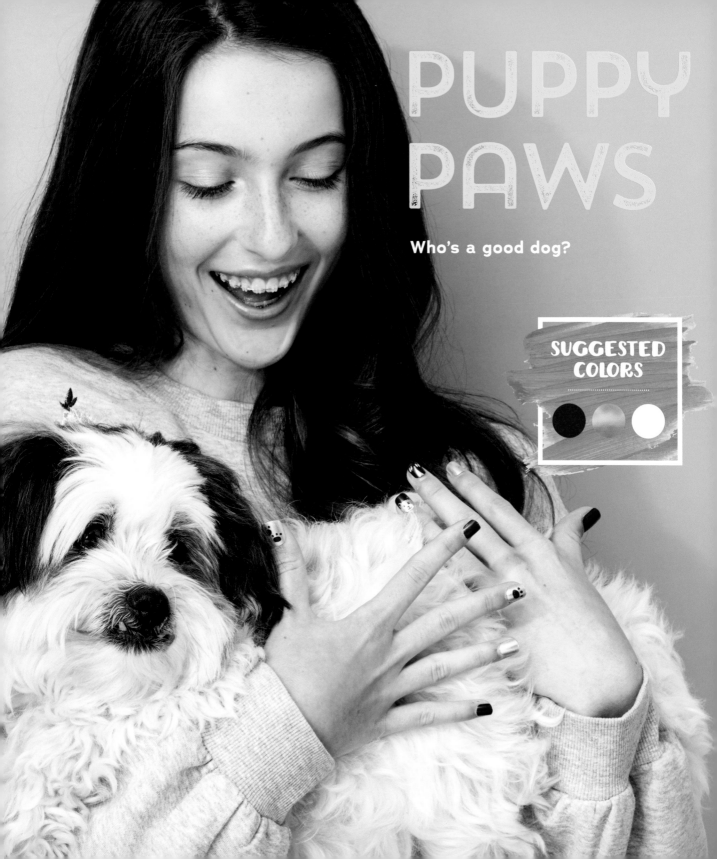

PUPPY PAWS

Who's a good dog?

SUGGESTED COLORS

Cute Pup

1 Paint a blue base coat (page 6) on two nails next to each other.

2 On one nail, draw a large gold half circle at the base of your nail, using the regular nail polish brush.

3 With the detail brush, draw two small nubs for ears.

4 Paint a small white half circle for the muzzle at the tip of your nail.

5 Using blue polish, paint the eyes, nose, mouth, and inner ear details.

6 **WAGGING TAIL** On the other nail, paint a curved gold line. Then add little white lines around the tail.

Paw Prints

1 Paint a gold base coat (page 6) on your nail.

2 Dot a large circle in the center. (On larger nails, you may be able to fit two paws.)

3 Add three little dots close to the circle.

MANI STYLE BOX

BEACH BEAUTY

Prepare for a tidal wave of compliments!

Ice Pop

1. Paint a purple base coat (page 6).

2. With the detail brush, paint an arch on your nail in green.

3. Add a short white line under the ice pop to make the stick, and two lines on the ice pop.

4. Finish your design by painting a teardrop drip (page 9) under your ice pop.

Beachy Waves

1 Paint the bottom part of your nail gold.

2 Then, paint the top part of your nail blue.

3 Use the detail brush to paint a white squiggle where the blue and gold meet.

4 Add some squiggly, horizontal white lines on the blue part of your nail for some waves.

ACCENT NAIL

Use the sun sticker to really add some summer fun to your mani.

Sparkly Starfish

1 Paint a blue base coat (page 6) on your nail. Add a few white squiggles.

2 Using the detail brush, paint five gold lines that meet in the middle.

MANI STYLE BOX

DAZZLING DESERT

Sparkle like a mirage.

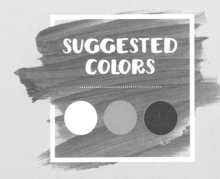

SUGGESTED COLORS

··· PRO TIP ···

On larger nails, you may be able to paint two cacti.

1 Paint a white base coat (page 6) on your nails.

2 Use the detail brush to paint a straight green line.

3 Add two small curved lines that connect with the first line.

4 Dot pink polish on top to create a cactus blossom.

MANI STYLE BOX

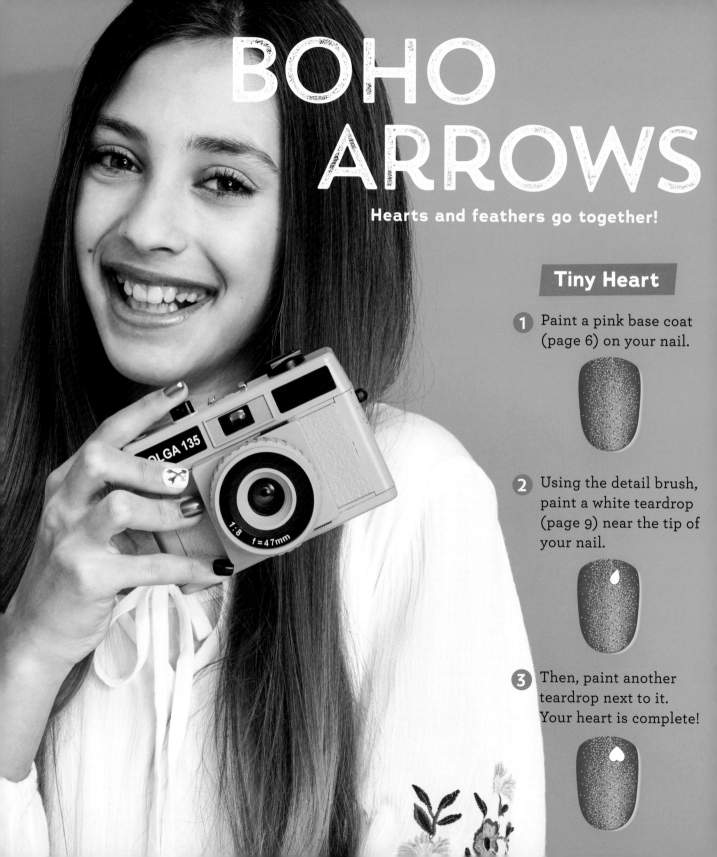

BOHO ARROWS

Hearts and feathers go together!

Tiny Heart

1 Paint a pink base coat (page 6) on your nail.

2 Using the detail brush, paint a white teardrop (page 9) near the tip of your nail.

3 Then, paint another teardrop next to it. Your heart is complete!

Arrows

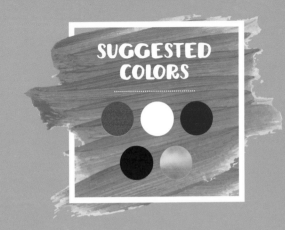

1. Paint a white base coat (page 6) on your nails.

2. Using the detail brush, paint two thin purple lines.

3. Add tiny pink hearts to opposite ends of each line.

4. Paint small purple marks on the other end.

··· PRO TIP ···
Draw crossed lines to make your arrows extra fancy.

Fancy Feather

1. With the detail brush, paint a curved blue line down the center of your nail.

2. Draw little lines in blue and gold, starting from the bottom of the line, and working your way up.

MANI STYLE BOX

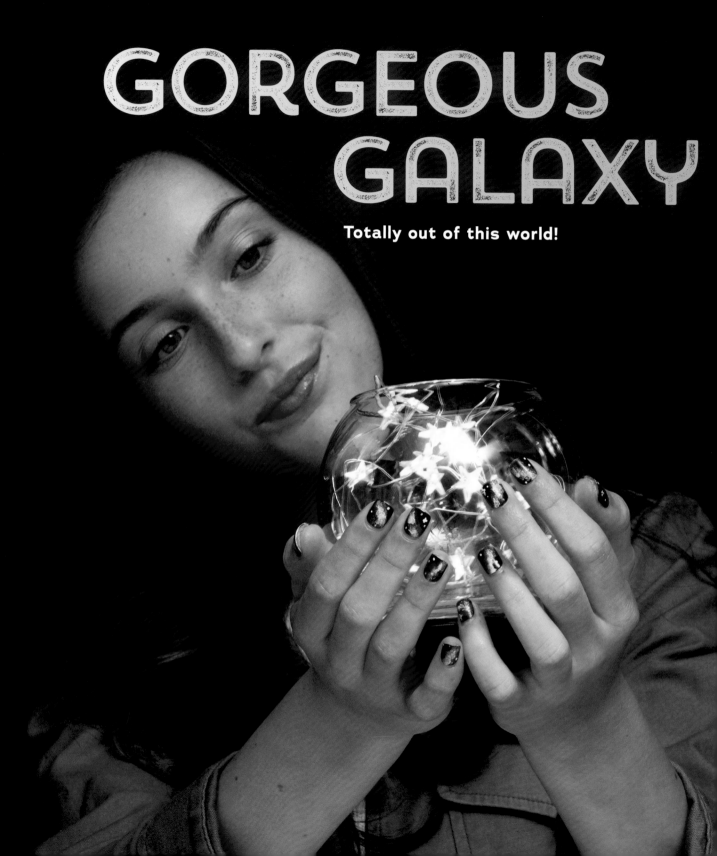

GORGEOUS GALAXY

Totally out of this world!

1 Paint a blue base coat (page 6) on your nails.

2 Snip off a small piece of your blender with scissors.

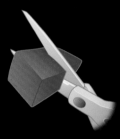

3 Use the blender snippet to dab purple polish on your nails. Dab lightly to avoid smudging.

4 Dab a tiny bit of white polish on your nail. A little polish goes a long way.

5 Repeat Step 4 with gold polish.

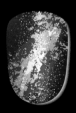

6 With the dotting tool, add white dots for stars. Cross two short lines to make an extra bright star.

SLIME TIME

The perfect balance of glam and gross.

SUGGESTED COLORS

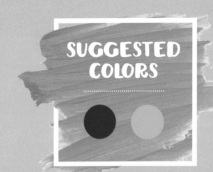

1 Paint a purple base coat (page 6) on your nails.

2 Paint a green line across the tip of your nail.

··· PRO TIP ···
You may need two coats of green polish to fully cover the purple base coat.

3 Add a few staggered dots below the green line.

4 Using the detail brush, connect the dots to the line to create drips. Try to curve the connecting lines to make your slime look goopy.

COLOR SWITCH
Paint a gold base coat and pink drips for a sparkly look.

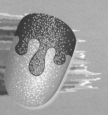

MYSTERIOUS MOON

Going through a phase?

SUGGESTED COLORS

Paint the moon phases in order, starting with the new moon on your pinky.

1 Paint a blue base coat (page 6) on your nails.

2 **FULL**
Use the detail brush and white polish to paint a circle on your nail. Don't make it perfect—gaps will look like craters.

3 **QUARTER**
Paint a half circle in white, like a C. Then fill in the shape, leaving it a little imperfect.

4 **CRESCENT**
Repeat Step 3, but only fill in a little bit of the C shape with white.

5 **SLIVER**
Paint a simple C shape, but do not fill it in.

6 **NEW MOON**
Leave the first nail blank for the "new moon." Dot a few stars and use the detail brush to add a few short lines.

MOON PHASES

The moon is "lit" because the sun's light bounces off the moon. Earth blocks some of the sun's light and casts a shadow on the moon. This shadow changes a bit every day, causing the moon to "wax" (grow bigger) or "wane" (grow smaller). There are eight phases of the moon, but you have 10 fingers, so we took some artistic license.

| New Moon | Waxing Crescent | First Quarter | Waxing Gibbous | Full | Waning Gibbous | Last Quarter | Waning Crescent |

OMBRÉ SHIMMER

When you can't decide between two colors— use both!

SUGGESTED COLORS

You will also need the polish blender. Petroleum jelly and a cottom swab may be useful, too.

1 Use a cotton swab to apply a thin layer of petroleum jelly on the skin around your nails. This will help you wipe away the extra nail polish later.

2 Paint a white base coat (page 6) on your nails. This will make the ombré pop.

3 Apply a generous stripe of gold polish to your blender, followed by a metallic pink stripe.

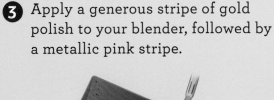

4 Roll the blender back and forth over your nail. Do not wipe or rub, as this will smudge the stripes together.

5 Repeat Steps 2–3 until you like the way your ombré looks.

6 When your nails are completely dry, wipe off the petroleum jelly with a paper towel. You can use your detail brush dipped in nail polish remover to get rid of any stray polish on your skin.

REUSING YOUR BLENDER

To clean your blender, just cut off the painted area with scissors to get a new flat surface. If you use up your blender, you can use cosmetic sponges, sold at drugstores.

FRESH FRUIT

A little slice of sweetness.

1. Paint an ombré design (page 40) using a wide pink stripe and a narrow green stripe.

2. Paint three blue teardrops for seeds.

SUGGESTED COLORS

You will also need the polish blender.

Rind

1. Paint a green base coat (page 6) on your nails.

ACCENT NAIL

Make a statement with decals on solid-colored nails.

2. Use the detail brush to paint a few white squiggles going up and down.

STUNNING SUNSET

Or sunrise, if you're an early bird.

1 Paint an ombré design (page 40) on your nails using pink and purple.

SUGGESTED COLORS

You will also need the polish blender.

2 Draw a curve across the base of your nail with blue.

3 Add three blue triangles using the detail brush.

ACCENT NAIL

Add a few bird decals flying across your nails.

UNICORN MAGIC

Sometimes you just need to get a little fancy!

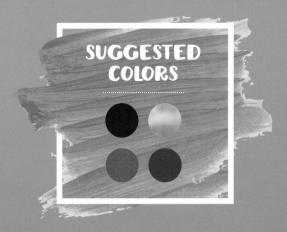

1 Using your polish brush, paint a blue diagonal stripe on the center of your bare nail.

2 Add a gold stripe above the blue.

3 Then, add a pink stripe above that.

4 Fill in any space under the blue line with purple.

5 Use your detail brush dipped in nail polish remover to get rid of any stray polish on your skin.

EXPERT OMBRÉ

Try painting an ombré nail (page 40) with these four colors: pink, green, blue, and purple.

Then, add a magical gold unicorn sticker!

CREDITS

DESIGNER: Vanessa Han

WRITER: Caitlin Harpin

TECHNICAL ILLUSTRATOR: Monika Roe

PACKAGE DESIGNER: Owen Keating

BUYER: Kelly Shaffer

PHOTOGRAPHERS: Michael Miranda and Aaron Dyer

PRODUCT DEVELOPMENT MANAGER: Gina Kim

PRODUCT DEVELOPMENT ASSISTANT: Kim Rogers

PRODUCT INTEGRITY SPECIALIST: Sam Walker

SPECIAL THANKS TO: Stacy Lellos, Netta Rabin, Hannah Rogge, April Chorba, and Henri Fluffleton

Get creative with more from KLUTZ

Looking for more goof-proof activities, sneak peeks, and giveaways? Find us online!

 KlutzCertified   KlutzCertified   KlutzCertified   KlutzCertified   Klutz

Klutz.com • thefolks@klutz.com • 1-800-737-4123